THE MINIMALIST BUDGET

SAVING MONEY AND SIMPLIFYING YOUR LIFE WITH A MINIMALIST LIFESTYLE ON A MINIMALIST BUDGET

By Damien Cash

I0463785

ISBN-13: 978-1502340658

ISBN-10: 1502340658

PRYDE
PUBLISHING

Why I Wrote This Book

When I finished university I began the tedious process of job-searching. I had been to several different countries with my family as a teenager and dreamed of having a job where I could carry on traveling. I consider myself to be a student of world cultures and love the excitement of being far away from home experiencing something new and interesting. Instead, I found myself sitting in the office of a banking firm trying to save enough cash to buy a home. After a few weeks I realized my home was not here anyway—it was "out there" where all the fun and excitement was. I made a major decision and, some would say, a major risk by giving up my position at the firm. I gave up my opportunity for job security to pursue what I had really wanted all along, which was to travel the world. I just knew that I would never be happy in my situation as it currently was because my dream was to travel; not sit around in a bank punching away on a computer.

I packed my bags and started looking for a way to fund myself while I travelled. But what could I do? This was my first hurdle. In university I had taken the wrong degree by majoring in business and social science because I had listened to the advice of society. These weren't exactly the kind of degrees that would enable me to travel unless I worked my way up to become a major international businessman. But I was years away from that and I never wanted to be a businessman anyway. I took a short 4-week course that would qualify me to teach English overseas and immediately went to Asia. I started off teaching for barely $800 a month in a small city out in the middle of nowhere. I was the only foreigner in town and got stared at everywhere I went. I felt like an alien in this place. Some could not believe that a young, intelligent, university-educated man would lower himself to this. Indeed, $800 per month was a far cry from my original plans when I was pursuing the typical middle-class lifestyle. But you know what? I was happy. As far as I was concerned, I was living the dream. Even though the cost of living in Asia was far cheaper than in my own country, I still had to operate on a tight budget. And this was my first lesson in minimalism.

I didn't have much but I was free, happy, and living the dream. I became a minimalist as a matter of necessity so that I could pursue the things that I really cared about. As my financial situation improved I still held to the minimalist philosophy that had brought me so far. I found that minimalism actually made me more productive and focused because I wasn't wasting my time on trivial things. Minimalism gave me more time and energy to devote to things that I wanted to do. I drove some of this newfound energy and productivity into projects that would allow me to retire from a normal job altogether. When I made the decision that day to pack my bags and leave everything behind, I made the best decision of my life. As a result of this decision I was forced into a minimalist mindset and I haven't looked back since. Minimalism has enabled me to retire faster than even an elusive corporate position would allow.

Now make no mistake, I am not asking you to leave everything behind and become a poor English teacher overseas. I tell you my story simply to demonstrate how I came to be a minimalist and how I came to see the benefits of the minimalist lifestyle. If you currently work in a corporate position and you're happy with your job, then by all means I would urge you to stay where you are. But I do want to ask you to consider a minimalist lifestyle so that you get even more out of life. If you have decided that you too want to see the benefits of minimalism—and having read this far I assume that you do—then I am here to help. During my time on the road I learned a lot about keeping a budget and saving money. Many people have come to me for advice since then and now I've decided to make a compilation of my strategies in this book. Here is a short summary of what you're going to learn:

- An overview of minimalism: What is the minimalist lifestyle? Why is minimalist living so popular? How can I benefit from minimalism?

- The minimalist mindset: How to break negativity and reconstruct a positive mindset with minimalism.

- The minimalist budget: Simplify your life and save money with a minimalist budget. Make life easier, become more productive, and save a lot of money in the process by learning the secrets of the minimalist budgeting strategy.

- Cutting down expenditures: Learn the most effective ways of cutting down your expenses without jeopardizing the quality of your life.

- Maintaining minimalism: Stay motivated and committed with simple strategies you can implement from day one.

I want to congratulate you on getting this book. I hope you enjoy it! It may just be one of the most important books you'll ever read about minimalism and budgeting. If this book helps you in any way, please take a minute of your time to post a review on Amazon. It would be much appreciated!

Damien Cash.

TABLE OF CONTENTS

BONUS: SUBSCRIBE FOR FREE BOOKS

We frequently promote our new releases by offering free books and discounts for a limited time as a "Thank You" to our customers. Subscribe to our list so that you do not miss out on these great offers!

Go here now to receive your FREE gift: thelifemasters.launchrock.com

To contact our authors, discuss their books or stay updated on their latest releases, please follow us on our social media pages:

Facebook: facebook.com/PrydePublishing

Twitter: twitter.com/PrydePublishing.

MINIMALISM: AN OVERVIEW

What is Minimalism?

Minimalism can mean different things to different people. This makes it difficult to give a short answer to the question of what minimalism is. Minimalism does not mean that you have to give up the comforts of modern technology or sell everything you own and become a monk. Although some minimalists may prefer to do so, most people in the 21st century would find this to be an extremely unhappy and unproductive lifestyle. Minimalist living is the exact opposite of this. Minimalism is all about leading a more productive, more focused, and more fulfilling life by simplifying and doing away with unnecessary distractions. Again, let me stress that the meanings of "simplifying" and "unnecessary distractions" are going to be different for everyone. There is no rule book for minimalism; only general principles that you can apply to your life according to your wants and needs. There are many different flavors of minimalism and you just have to experiment to see what works for you.

If you follow one tip and find that things just aren't working for you, no one is going to stop you from tweaking your original plan. Even so, I would recommend you put your best foot forward and make an effort to live outside of your comfort zone. I never would have thought that living a single day without television was humanly possible. People rely on television for so many things these days—entertainment, news, and even education. But living in countries with no English-language television channels, I had to quickly learn to adapt. This changed my perspective on the necessity of owning a television and I felt all the better for it. For the sake of my family there is now a television set in the household but I still refuse to watch it. Sometimes I'll sit down for a few minutes and catch a glimpse while I'm eating dinner or something and it just reinforces my beliefs about television. I was watching a news channel one time and thought that I had stumbled across a comedy sketch because I found the way that they presented their views to be absolutely hilarious. Even dramas became unbearable by how out of touch with reality they seemed.

Again, I'm not asking you to give up your television if you feel you need it. For what it's worth, I became a Breaking Bad fanatic and ordered the entire series, which I watched in one sitting over three days without sleeping. And that is minimalism at its finest. I learned to appreciate a good television show even more because I no longer watch television for the sake of passing some time or relaxing. I've learned to pass time and relax in other, more productive ways. All I'm asking is that you make an effort to try something new, even if it doesn't work out for you, because you may just find that you've made a good decision and improved the quality of your life.

Why Minimalism? The Benefits

Minimalists firmly believe in the concept that less is more and strongly view the notion of "quality over quantity" as an important element in the minimalist lifestyle. But how can less be more? As I mentioned in the introduction, I was essentially force-fed minimalism when I decided to pursue my dreams of traveling. I had to quickly adapt to a tight budget but I soon realized that my quality of life had improved significantly. Minimalist living enabled me to sharpen my focus and increase productivity. I had more free time than I knew what to do with and most of this energy was channeled into projects that allowed me to retire at a young age.

Minimalism is about emptying your life of distractions and things that don't matter to make room for the things that do—

you throw out everything that slows you down both mentally and physically. In general, this is going to make you more focused, more productive, and more able to pursue your interests, dreams, and passions. Decision-making on trivial matters is minimized and mental energy is expended in more important areas of your life. Many people are attracted to minimalism for financial reasons and, while there is no harm in that, I always found the financial benefits to simply be the icing on the cake. Having more money in the wallet naturally follows the minimalist lifestyle.

Another natural result of minimalism is reduced stress levels. When your expenditures are out of control it can have nasty consequences. Things such as depression, divorce, and even suicide are often linked to financial struggles. Having your finances under control lifts a huge burden that you no longer need to worry about, which will make you less stressed and more able to enjoy life the way you want to.

Minimalism vs Frugalism

Although there are many overlaps between minimalism and frugal living, they are two distinct concepts with some important differences. Frugalism, also known as thriftiness, is more concerned with trying to get more value out of your money rather than living a minimalist lifestyle. In fact, some frugalists may even horde things if they think it will save them money in the future. They like to consider all possible ways of getting things for free and keep an eye on the best deals that they can get for their money. By contrast, minimalists are concerned with simplifying their life and decluttering. They are typically against hording and aren't always looking for ways to be frugal. A minimalist might choose to spend a good amount of money on a product if they think it will make them more productive and will eliminate more, less-efficient things from their life.

This is not to say that these two philosophies aren't compatible. Many minimalists use frugalism to supplement their lifestyle and vice versa. As a matter of fact, minimalism by its very nature could be seen as encouraging frugality. However, let me stress that this book is not going to be primarily focused on thriftiness because, with minimalist living, thriftiness is not always seen as the best option. For instance, buying several pairs of cheap shoes probably doesn't cut it for a minimalist. Instead, they might prefer to buy only one pair of good quality shoes that aren't going to wear down and turn into a pair of flip-flops within a week or two.

What is Minimalist Budgeting?

Whenever I mention the word "budget" throughout this book, I want you to think "spending plan" instead. Not only is a spending plan a more friendly way of thinking about a budget, it also better reflects the principles of minimalist living. For most people, a "budget" conjures up images of having a plan that dictates what, when, and where you spend. They start entering the early stages of depression as they envision a future of two-minute noodles and second-hand clothing. Thinking back to their days as a poor student at college, a budget doesn't exactly sound very appealing anymore.

So, what is a minimalist budget? How does it differ from a spending plan? There is nothing written in stone with minimalism because everyone has different lifestyles, expenses, and needs. A spending plan allows you to control how your money is used and allocated. It recognizes that expenses will inevitably change from month to month. By contrast, most people don't want to "budge" their "budget". Unfortunately, this often leads to a failed budgeting strategy when things don't work out and they begin to give up on their carefully-planned budget. This is not to say that I don't approve of a budget plan as they are traditionally understood—if it works for you then that's totally fine.

My hope for you, the reader, is to develop a spending plan that caters to your own unique circumstances, needs, and wants. The only thing I would urge you to commit to is commitment itself. A spending plan is only as good as your commitment to it. In later chapters we will cover a few simple ways that can help you maintain your motivation and commitment to your minimalist budget.

THE MINIMALIST MINDSET

Before approaching anything in life it's important to have the correct mindset. So the first and most fundamental step in the direction of minimalism is to begin working on changing your mindset. Am I asking you to brainwash yourself? No, well... a little positive brainwashing can't hurt. Changing the way you think about things isn't always a bad thing. In fact, it is often the most important step that we take towards creating a better life. I've broken this process down into two parts. Remember, developing a more positive, minimalist mindset is always going to be a work in progress.

Destroying a Negative Mindset: Decluttering the Mind

Since you're reading this book I have to assume that you are already prepared to move forward with a minimalist lifestyle and have changed your mindset accordingly. Yet some people still find themselves holding back despite their good intentions. If you find yourself in this camp I want you to ask yourself what exactly it is that prevents you from taking action. For many people it usually comes down to one of the following:

1) You've tried budgeting before. You have every book in existence on saving money but despite your best efforts you simply aren't achieving the results that you were hoping for. It's been over a month and you still haven't become a millionaire.

2) Although it looks good on paper, you just can't bring yourself to take action because of doubts in the back of your mind or a lack of motivation to follow through with your plans.

3) You've had some great success in the past but can't seem to progress any further. You feel as though you have

reached some sort of plateau and can't take it to the next level.

People are led to these dangerous beliefs because of two primary reasons. The first reason is that we often set self-imposed limits into our thinking from a young age. Knowingly or unknowingly, your parents, teachers, and other people throughout your life may have influenced these self-imposed limits. Perhaps it was even your own doing. In school, I was the worst speller in my class. I had to take special lessons to get me up to speed with the other students but had come to the conclusion that maybe writing just wasn't my thing—to put it bluntly, I sucked and was sure that I would probably lose a spelling contest to a drunken chimp. Fortunately, I had a great teacher and mentor during those lessons who was able to motivate me to achieve more. I eventually became the best speller in my class and even corrected the teacher's spelling on several occasions, much to his embarrassment! But had I focused on the fact that I was a terrible speller I would still be the same today. Unfortunately, too many people go down this path.

The second major reason is that people set unrealistic goals and can't appreciate the small victories. We always want to be the best at something but when progress is slow we lose motivation. This is only going to sabotage a positive outcome. By having unrealistic expectations we set ourselves up for disappointment and don't appreciate what's in front of us and the progress that we actually have made. This is a big reason why I like to think of a budget as a spending plan because it gives me more freedom to change things around as needed and doesn't lead to disappointment when I haven't saved the amount of money that my budget dictated would be available.

To summarize, you need to think about the following:

- Remove your self-imposed inner-beliefs that limit your possibilities.

- Try not to set unrealistic goals or have unrealistic expectations.

- Appreciate the small victories without losing sight of the big picture.

- Begin the process of building a more positive mindset.

- Focus on positive outcomes instead of your problems.

Building a Positive Mindset

Changing your way of thinking isn't always an easy thing to do; old habits die hard. But you first need to be willing to make an effort to change. If you've already begun the process of removing the negative beliefs that limit your success then this shouldn't be an issue. When your problems become more important than your goals you begin to lose hope. By focusing on your goals you begin to see the solutions to your problems much more clearly. And the number one thing that holds us back from achieving our financial goals, despite having a positive mindset, is something I call needless needs.

It's amazing how unimportant certain things become when you have no money. But when people have more money, they suddenly have more needs and wants. Many people that I know find themselves in this category. No matter how much money they make, they can't seem to save any of it. When they're making $40,000 per year they don't save anything and when they start making $80,000 per year they still aren't saving anything. They move into a bigger house, buy more consumer luxuries, eat out at restaurants more often, and still can't figure out why their bank account is just as empty as when they were making $40,000.

In short, more money often gives rise to more needless needs. Things that you had previously never even thought you wanted suddenly get bumped to the top of your wish-list. The reasons for this phenomenon are many. From a young age we are attracted to the idea that owning more things is a good thing. This especially rings true for people who were raised in families that didn't have much. We may also be manipulated by advertising, consumerism, and so on. Others may simply have an obsession with keeping up with the Jones's, making sure that no one dares spend more money than they do. In the end, all of these things distract you from achieving your goals and make you less productive than you would like to be—more expenses and more items means you waste more money and time.

Until you recognize this obvious but often overlooked element of your spending habits, your carefully-planned budget is almost as good as useless. I've known millionaires who have ended up dirt-broke because they either failed or refused to recognize that their spending habits were financially unviable. A good friend of mine won over a million dollars in the lottery, *twice*—no one could believe his luck. After several years of living the high-life his luck ran out and he drove himself into debt trying to sponsor a lifestyle he could no longer afford. It seems like an amazingly stupid mistake that only a certified moron would be capable of achieving. Yet is the average Joe that much better? As it turns out, not really. I think it's safe to say that most of us are guilty of pursuing a lifestyle that we can't actually afford. And in a world where credit cards and loans seem to grow on trees, it's an easy trap to fall into.

A minimalist is able to recognize these shortcomings and builds a game-plan that caters to their situation. Creating this game-plan, and the mindset that allows us to follow through with that plan, begins by asking ourselves the following questions:

-   Am I ready to create a more positive mindset?

- Have I eliminated the negative beliefs that hold me back?

- What am I trying to achieve? What are my goals?

- Why do I want to achieve these goals?

- How can I ensure that I will achieve them?

- Can I steer clear of the "needless needs" trap?

Once you have answered these questions to yourself honestly, you'll be amazed how easily a positive mindset follows—just as I had discovered as a struggling English teacher in Asia when everything I owned could fit into a single suitcase.

CUTTING DOWN YOUR EXPENDITURES

Before you start working on developing your budget, it might help if you can begin thinking of ways to cut down your expenditures. And no, I'm not going to tell you that you have to become single again or start eating only one meal a day but feel free to do so at your own risk. In fact, in minimalist thinking, cutting down expenditures might even mean spending more on something if it is going to be better in the long-term. It's also important to remember that expenditures aren't always financial. There are many types of expenditures: mental expenditures, physical expenditures, financial expenditures, time expenditures, and so on.

Any change in one type of expenditure is going to cause a ripple effect across all other areas too. After doing the math you need to figure out what works best for you and what your priority is at any single moment. Since you've chosen this book I have to assume that financial expenditures have become a top priority for you. The beauty of minimalism is that it has the ability to cut expenditures in every single area with one fell swoop. I've broken this chapter down into four sections to show you just a few ways that can help to dramatically decrease your expenditures.

Quality vs Quantity

I know I've already mentioned it but I'll reiterate once again the importance of understanding quality and quantity. Both of these terms a pretty straightforward—quality generally means that something is of higher value whereas quantity means having more of something. The reason that minimalists generally favor quality over quantity is because owning more of something is a direct contradiction to our goals. I have already given the analogy of owning one pair of quality shoes versus owning five pairs of cheap bad-quality shoes. It may surprise you but this favoring of quality not only helps maintain a minimalist lifestyle; it can also cut down your expenditures.

Quality items usually cost a lot more but will last for a much longer period of time. In addition, cheap items don't always turn out to be so cheap once you factor in the maintenance and repair costs that you have to account for over time. Now don't get me wrong, cheap items are not always bad-quality. And not everyone will be able to afford to replace everything in their house with a superior-quality version. It's entirely up to you how you wish to balance quality and quantity. It may sound unusual that I encourage you to spend more money in a book about minimalism and budgeting but there are a few very good reasons why this is going to benefit you in the long run.

Firstly, you're buying quality items that should last longer. Secondly, you may be spending more on an item but you should be buying less. And thirdly, as a consequence of the previous two points, you should be evaluating your purchases more carefully and making better decisions about what you want to buy. This is going to make you appreciate your possessions much more than you did before and make it less likely that you'll waste money on items you don't need.

Keep in mind that there is no need to go over the top. You don't need a $1000 dress to impress the boys or a $600 pair of shoes to protect your feet. All you need is something simple, affordable, and good-quality. If you're one of those people that have an obsession with expensive fashions and excessive spending just to impress the people around you, you're probably reading the wrong book because budgeting is never going to work for you—unless you're prepared to change.

Seeking Alternatives

Another great method of cutting down your expenditures is by seeking cheaper alternatives to things you already have. Before making any purchase it would be wise to ask yourself if there are any cheaper alternatives available that still maintain the quality you're after. In the digital age, many of the more-expensive physical products have been replaced by much cheaper digital alternatives. In fact, most of you are probably reading this on a Kindle device right now. Printed material such as newspapers and books are rapidly being replaced by the digital universe.

If you don't own a computer and an internet connection you're probably doing yourself a huge disservice. With this setup you can make your bill payments online; download digital books; research for your essays and projects; watch your favorite TV shows; listen to music; connect with friends and family; have an online job and the list just goes on. It used to be a funny joke to consider the idea of downloading cars and guns from the internet. But the advent of 3D printing has since made this into a reality and is maturing very quickly. As you can see, telephones, televisions, and a host of other things are rapidly going the way of the horse and carriage.

Some things simply cannot be displaced with digital versions. Although it would be nice, we're still a long way from being able to plug into our laptops and get in our daily work-out. But a good alternative to an expensive gym membership would be to save the money and put it towards creating your own home-gym setup. You might also want to ditch the car for public transport, which is sometimes faster anyway if you're taking a railway system and avoiding all of that traffic. You could even start walking and biking—you might get rid of both the gym membership and the car doing that!

If you want to buy an iPad, you could consider any of the cheaper alternatives on the market that are still good-quality products, such as a Nexus. If you're after some expensive software for your computer, you can often find free or open-source alternatives. For example, Microsoft Office could be replaced with OpenOffice, which is an absolutely free office suite that is compatible with documents made in Microsoft Office. If you're looking to save on utilities, consider installing an LED lighting setup—it's much cheaper than traditional lighting methods and will save you a lot of money in the long-term. Sometimes there simply is no alternative or maybe the alternative isn't suited to your tastes. But it's always wise to weigh your options.

Even rare luxuries like a vacation can have a good alternative. Instead of getting an expensive hotel and eating at restaurants you could go camping and take your own food. I used to go camping with my family a lot as a child and in hindsight it was probably because my parents couldn't afford much else. But some of my best memories come from this time. This is in stark contrast to the hotels I've stayed at over the past decade, most of which I can't even remember.

Decluttering and Eliminating

Nothing says minimalism better than getting rid of the unnecessary things in your home and life. Since this book is not about this particular aspect of minimalism I'll keep it short. Decluttering your house and removing the things you don't really use or need can make you money and save you money. You can sell the items or donate them. If you sell them you're making some money but either way you're still going to save. It's amazing how many people buy and own things they don't use. These items are kind of like my children; they sit around for years doing not much of anything and eat up a large chunk of my income while I hope they come in useful at some point. Of course, I can't simply declutter my children out of my life but I can get rid of that car I don't use but still have to wash and maintain every day. And the same goes for you. There may very well be things in your life that you don't use but are costing you money just by their very presence.

There's never a shortage of things that can be eliminated from life. I used to be a heavy cigarette smoker until I realized it was doing nothing except slowly killing me and wasting my money. Alcohol was never my vice because it just makes me tired but it was for some people around me. They had to buy beer every week and it just became another unnecessary expense for them. I was also a huge fan of soft drinks but I slowly came to like water. It wasn't easy but I don't really think much about it now and I still have a can of soda every now and then. This wasn't really my choice anyway because my dentist gave me a big lecture about the evils of soda and what it was doing to my teeth. In any case, you should start making a list of things that need to be eliminated from your life and your household. These unnecessary expenditures can make a huge difference on the bank account.

Supplementing Minimalism

In the overview, we briefly discussed thriftiness and frugalism and how this is sometimes used by minimalists to supplement their way of living. If you were attracted to minimalism for financial reasons then you may also want to supplement this with money-saving methods such as thriftiness. In my book *Life Hacks for the Aspiring Prodigy* is a chapter on how to save money, which you will get to preview at the end of this book. You'll see that there are many ways to save money besides planning a budget.

One time-tested method of saving money is to collect coupons. But as I've mentioned in my other book, collecting coupons from newspapers is a waste of time since you can find all the coupons you want online. Being aware of sales, discounts, and deals is also another well-known strategy of saving money. You should also know the right times to buy—sales and discounts often occur during holiday seasons or shortly afterwards when shops are clearing out the last of their stock.

In addition to these frugal measures are the plain, common-sense ideas that can save you money. Cook your own meals instead of eating out at restaurants that charge you five times as much for the same dish; plant your own vegetable garden so that you reduce your reliance on supermarkets; and move to an area within walking distance of the basic necessities you'll need throughout the week. The possibilities are only limited by your imagination so start thinking big. Since this is not a book about thriftiness I'm going to move on to strategies that you can use to plan your budget. If you're more interested in this subject you may want to buy any of the number of books out there on frugal living or check out my other book, which contains many useful money-saving hacks for everyday living.

THE MINIMALIST BUDGET

The Number-One Reason People Fail

Trying to save money is like trying to lose weight because the rules are simple but many fail. And the rule is this: to lose weight you have to eat less and exercise more and to save money you have to spend less and save more. Common-sense? Yes. Common? No. If you're spending more money than you're bringing home, you aren't going to save anything and that's the bottom-line. No matter how much you pray, no matter how much mental-gymnastics you perform, the math just won't add up. The main problem is that people spend more than they make and drive themselves into debt. As I've already mentioned, any Tom, Dick and Harry can do this, so can a millionaire, and so can you. And so the first step towards developing a solid spending plan is to figure out how much money you actually take home per month and what your monthly expenses are.

Tracking Expenses

To work out your expenses you will need to set aside at least an entire month to track where your money is going. This will be the longest but also the most important part of developing your budget. You can write this down into a journal or make a spreadsheet on Excel; the point is to track your expenditures. Obviously, your expenses will vary from month to month but it's a useful starting point. I would advise that you separate the month into four weeks to see if a pattern emerges. You might to choose to go for longer; two months, six months, one year, it doesn't matter. You need to track your expenses and find a general pattern that gives you a good idea of where your money is going. Here are a few expenses you might have:

- Rent

- Utilities

- Credit cards

- Food

- Insurance

- Gasoline

- Student loan

- Cell phone

This list should be further separated into two categories: *absolute expenses* and *discretionary expenses*. Absolute expenses are things that will require a chunk of your income every month—no questions asked. Examples include things like credit cards and loans, food, rent, internet, cable TV, and so on. It's always good to review your assumptions about what your necessary-expenses include because sometimes we can confuse the things we want with the things we need. Discretionary expenses are everything else: eating out, gifts, shopping, entertainment, charity, etc.

Review your expenses to see if there is any expenditure that can be reduced or even completely removed. If you've tracked your expenses correctly you should be able to pinpoint categories where you are overspending. Use the previous chapter on cutting down your expenditures as a guide to see if there are any ways you can reduce your expenses. You should focus on the discretionary expenses column in particular because this is where the majority of your overspending is likely to occur. That doesn't mean your absolute expenses category doesn't include overspending. Cable TV and internet aren't necessarily absolute expenses but they have become an absolute expense because of the way you've organized your life. Food and utilities are important but maybe you're spending more than you really need to. And perhaps you don't really need cable TV or the internet. Personally, I find that I do need the internet because it's become the primary source of my income and has been able to replace other expenses in my life (buying CDs and physical books, for instance).

Some people find that, no matter how hard they try, they either cannot seem to save any of their money or are saving less than what they expected. Even when they track their budget they can't see where they went wrong. What this often comes down to is unplanned expenses that weren't factored in when you were tracking your expenses. This could be anything from toilet paper and cleaning products to a car servicing. If you cannot be sure that you've accounted for every single expense imaginable or you're saving less than expected, you should add another category to your expenditures: unplanned expenses. In fact, you should add this category even if you aren't one of these people because even if you don't have an unplanned expense it just means that you're going to be saving more than expected at the end of the month. This could act as a vital morale-booster that motivates you to carry on towards your goals.

The Simple Minimalist Budget

Before you go ahead with planning your budget, you should try to make it a priority to eliminate your financial obligations. Make a list of expenses you would like to eliminate and use that as a guide for planning your budget. Here's an example:

- Credit card debts

- House payments

- Car payments

- Student loan

- Cable TV

- Other miscellaneous items, debts, and junk

A *minimalist* budget should be both simple and effective. After all, that's what minimalism is for. Now here's what a basic minimalist spending plan looks like:

- Net monthly income – monthly absolute expenses = money I can save or spend on whatever I want.

That's it! This simple formula is what I have used to save money for a long time. But there are a few benefits and other things that separate this from a traditional budget:

1) Expenses have been reduced because of the way that a minimalist organizes their life.

2) Fixed costs (absolute expenses) are unlikely to change from month to month. Therefore, we aren't going to be tracking individual expenses each day because we only have to worry about discretionary expenses and the amount remaining at the end of the month.

3) It sorts needs from wants and absolute expenses from discretionary expenses. After completing this calculation, everything left over is discretionary income—money to be saved or used at your discretion.

4) We already have an idea of our discretionary income and what needs to be changed. When you were tracking your expenses you may have surprised yourself to see just how little discretionary income you actually have. This might reveal the reason that you struggle to save money.

5) The spending plan is so simple that you could get your pet dog to manage it. You're not going to be spending valuable time working out how much money needs to be spent on milk and coffee because everything is included in your absolute expenses, which you tracked for a

month. Maintaining this spending plan literally takes only minutes of your time.

The 50/20/30 Method

Some people prefer a more structured approach to budgeting. The 50/20/30 method offers structure without become overly complicated like the more traditional budgets. Not everyone can, or will, adhere to the 50/20/30 "rule" but it's a helpful guide for people new to budgeting or those looking for a little structure. The 50/20/30 method is as follows.

1) 50% of your income: absolute expenses.

It sounds like a lot but since you've already tracked your absolute expenses you should have a pretty good idea of how much of your income actually goes towards your necessary expenditures. So at the start of each month, you should automatically set aside 50% of your cash flow to use on your absolute expenses. Let me repeat, absolute expenses are fixed costs that you have to pay: rent, utilities, transportation, etc.

2) 20% of your income: financial obligations.

Financial obligations should be your second most important priority. This includes things such as paying off debts and loans or even creating a retirement and an emergency savings account. I realize that a credit card debt could be considered an absolute expense but, for the purposes of this method, it's a category all on its own. That's because having to pay back a debt isn't exactly essential to your well-being in the way that buying food is. Taking control of your financial obligations is important if you want to get ahead, save more money, and avoid a 200 pound debt-collector. Once your debts are paid off you'll have more discretionary income, which leads us to our next category.

3) 30% of your income: discretionary expenses.

This is money that can be used at your discretion. You might choose to put it straight into a savings account or use it to finance your lifestyle choices. In the modern world, some luxuries have almost taken on a mandatory status. How many people could live without a cell phone these days? It's a discretionary expense but it has also become such an important part of life for most of us. Other discretionary expenses include eating out and gym memberships. If you're determined to rid yourself of debt, you should consider funneling some of your discretionary income back in to your financial obligations.

Remember, don't take the 50/20/30 "rule" too literally. It's only a framework for you to work with. Since you've already tracked your expenses, perhaps you've found that absolute expenses only take up 40% of your income. In that case, you may want to use a 40/30/30 ratio or a 40/40/20 ratio. It's entirely up to you.

Setting Goals

You should know by now that I consider goal-setting to be one of the most important things you can do to get ahead in life. The reason is really quite simple: if you don't have any goals it's likely that you don't have a plan either. And when you don't have a plan you're just walking around aimlessly without a clue as to what direction you want to move in. Setting goals is a very simple and even enjoyable part of the spending-plan process. There are two simple goal-setting strategies that I personally like to use:

1) Setting a few high goals that you expect to achieve over an extended period of time.

2) Setting several or more basic, simple goals that you expect to achieve within a relatively shorter period of time.

At the end of the day it's up to you if you want to use this template for setting your own goals but please remember what I said about setting realistic goals and appreciating the small victories. Having *high* goals doesn't necessarily mean having *unrealistic* goals; it means having high goals that are realistically achievable within a realistic period of time. Remember that surpassing a goal is always much better than not achieving it. I think you'll find that most people who have achieved great things did so without having such expectations initially. Movie stars didn't start their career expecting to be a celebrity and billionaires didn't start their businesses expecting to be super-rich.

To put this into perspective, let me give you an example. Mark Zuckerberg started Facebook "for fun" from his dormitory room at Harvard University. The small, relatively insignificant site carried photos of the school's students who could vote on who was "hotter". The site eventually blew up and spread to other universities. At some point, Zuckerberg realized the potential of his idea and dropped out of Harvard to devote himself to the development of Facebook full-time. By the age of 23 he was already a billionaire. Moral of the story? Don't try to be Superman; try to be Mark Zuckerberg.

Final Tips

If you would like to track your expenses in something like Excel but don't know how to use it, you can find a number of templates online. Just search for "simple budget template excel" or "budget template word", for example. Simply punch in your expense categories and the amounts, and you're done. I'll give you a couple of templates to get started. You can find a budget template for Excel and OpenOffice at these links:

http://office.microsoft.com/en-us/templates/simple-monthly-budget-TC103428920.aspx

http://templates.openoffice.org/en/search/node/budget

To simplify things even further, you should think about automating your life in as many ways as possible. Set up automatic payments online for bills that aren't going to change from month to month and consider opting in for paperless statements, if possible. You can also schedule automatic deliveries for products that you know you're always going to use—toilet paper and coffee, for example. Amazon.com, among others, offers this service. As an added bonus, many retailers offer discounts if you commit to a regular delivery schedule.

If you want to track your expenses using an online service instead of writing everything out in a journal or Excel file, I would highly recommend Mint.com. After taking the time to set up your account, Mint brings all your financial accounts together in one place and allows you to monitor your expenses, categorize transactions, set goals, and set a budget. And it does all of these things automatically. Oh, and it's free. Yeah, I like free stuff (who doesn't?) so here are a few other honorable mentions:

Personalcapital.com

Yodlee.com

Smartypig.com

Neobudget.com

Manageme.in

Maintaining Minimalism: The Lifestyle, The Commitment, and the Budget

List Your Items

Committing to a minimalist lifestyle won't be easy for everyone. Some people can get away with the set-and-forget approach but others need to discipline themselves. This doesn't mean you have to whip yourself with a belt but by using a few simple strategies that help you to plan and track your progress you should be able to maintain your commitment better.

The minimalist lifestyle states that less is more and that quality is almost always better than quantity. If you're already a minimalist you may have already done this but it never hurts to get a friendly reminder. Make a list and count every item that you own. You should update this list as needed when you buy new things or get rid of old items. Whenever possible, replace items rather than add to them. The goal here is to keep things to a minimum and reduce the hording mentality. If you're going to add to your list by buying a new item, try to get something that is good-quality and will last for a while, if you can afford to do so. Keeping a list of items might also reveal things about your budget that you hadn't seen before. So get a pen and paper, and start counting!

Set Realistic Goals

Here I come again with the goal-setting. Having realistic goals keeps you on track and makes it more likely for you to commit to your budget. They give you something to look forward to and something to work towards. I like to have few high goals or numerous simple goals. The first would be long-term goals and the second would be short-term goals. It's always good to have both long and short-term goals. If you only have long-term goals you may begin to feel demoralized that you haven't achieved them yet. If you only have short-term goals, you might be limiting your possibilities and potential.

The advantage of short-term goals is that progress is going to seem rapid since they can be achieved in a relatively short period of time. This will feel greatly rewarding and will make you keen to carry on pursuing your goals further. But whether long-term or short-term, your goals have to be realistic. With unrealistic expectations you set yourself up for disappointment and even failure. Therefore, you want your goals to be in line with your spending plan.

If you own 900 items, you may want to set a goal of getting down to 850 within a couple of months. What you don't want to do is try to go from 900 to 200 by the end of the week. It's simply an unrealistic goal unless you've spent most of your life hording crap and rummaging through dump sites. Likewise, don't try to set the goal of becoming the next Bill Gates by the end of the year when your annual income is only $40,000. Becoming a millionaire is a perfectly realistic long-term goal if you have a good long-term strategy. And depending on your cash flow, becoming a millionaire might even be a short-term goal for some of you. The key here is to *get real*.

Record Your Accomplishments

Recording your accomplishments can be a huge motivator because it shows the progress you've made and demonstrates just how far you've come. There are a number of ways to do this. Ideally, you want to do this publicly because going public has the added benefit of making you want to stick to your goals; no one wants to fail when everyone is looking at you! There are several ways that you can go public. It could be as simple as sending out a tweet on Twitter or updating your Facebook status.

If you're game, you can vlog (video blog) about your progress using Youtube or some other video medium. You could also set up an actual blog and write about it. If you're a private person, you can write things down in a journal for reference over time. Whatever the case, it's always good to look back and wow yourself. This will keep you motivated and keep you committed.

Quarterly Audits

It's a good idea to reevaluate your spending plan every three months or so for at least two reasons. Firstly, a review of your expenditures might reveal some expenses you think you might be able to remove or reduce. After a period of time, you might decide that cable TV isn't as important as it used to be or maybe you've finally paid back your student loan. Secondly, expenses will inevitably change from time to time. Perhaps you got a pay rise at work and now have more money to direct towards financial obligations or discretionary expenses. Or maybe you've recently suffered an injury and need to add medical expenses to your budget. In any case, it's important that your spending plan is reviewed every three months if not immediately.

When it comes to things like cable TV and other subscription services, a good tip is to move it from the absolute expenses category into the discretionary expenses category at a time when you feel ready. That way, you've begun to realize that it isn't a necessary expense and you can begin to take steps towards eliminating it from your life. If you already done this when you were tracking your expenses then great—you're well on your way to living a minimalist lifestyle and saving money!

In addition, you should audit your list of items for similar reasons. You may have forgotten to do so over the months and you might find things on your list that are no longer needed. Or perhaps you got rid of something that you need back in your life again because you couldn't live without it. Update your list accordingly and review it again in three months.

And finally, you should review your goals. If your expenses have changed, your goals are likely to change also. This keeps you on track and keeps your goals realistic.

Conclusion

You now have all the tools and information you need to begin developing a successful spending plan and living a more meaningful and productive life. But the only way that you will succeed is by taking action and committing yourself to each step along the way. This begins by removing negative belief systems that you may have and working on building a more positive mindset. Be grateful for every inch of progress you make and focus on your goals instead of your problems. This is the first step in creating a successful minimalist budget.

As you begin to develop your spending plan you need to be aware of imaginary needs that pop up from time to time. Some people are addicted to fast-food just as much as others are addicted to drugs. It seems irrational to those around them because it's an imaginary need that most of us live without just fine. But to the individual it's very real. That's why it can be difficult for us to separate needs from imaginary needs and wants. Remembering the story of the poor millionaire reminds me of how easy it can be to fall in to this trap.

As you track your expenses you should be able to see whether or not you have any of these imaginary needs or if you're overspending in certain areas where you could cut down. You don't need to live like a monk or a prisoner but, if you're like most people, you should see at least a few areas where there is room for some change. You can cut down your expenditures by seeking alternatives to what you currently use, going for quality over quantity, eliminating unnecessary things from your life, and with good old consumer-conscious thriftiness.

Try to keep your budget as simple as possible. Poring over insignificant details often leads people to abandon their spending plan and their goals. I have no problem with traditional budgeting methods but I personally found through trial and error that they limit my potential. Now some people may prefer these types of budgets and, if you're one of these people, simply adjust your budget accordingly. I'm sure you'll still be able to find something to take away from this book.

Whether you set long-term or short-term goals, make sure that they are realistic. Having unrealistic expectations brings disappointment whereas surpassing realistic goals brings even more determination to succeed. I also highly recommend that you record your progress and accomplishments—either publicly or privately. Being able to look back at where it all began will be a huge motivator for you in the future.

Don't forget to review your budget and goals on a regular basis. Your income, expenses and goals are likely to change from time to time. As you progress down the path of minimalism you may also find that your needs and wants have also changed. Let me also remind you again that nothing in this book is sacred; it is only a guide. Every person is unique and every person has unique circumstances.

Thank you again for getting this book. Remember, knowledge is power. If the information in this book was enjoyable or helpful in any way, please take the time to share your thoughts and post a review on Amazon. And don't forget to sign up for your free gift at thelifemasters.launchrock.com

To your success,

Damien Cash.

PREVIEW OF *"LIFE HACKS FOR THE ASPIRING PRODIGY"*

Chapter 2: Money Hacks

Get A Cheap Car

Looking for a cheap car? Need to save money? Yeah, me too. Well here's a tip that can help you get the upper hand and save some cash the next time you're arguing with a car dealer. Wait until the end of the month and then take a walk to your nearest car dealership (don't worry, you'll be driving back home). If the month has been slow for them, they will gladly take a loss to meet their quota.

Stop Touching Things!

Did you know you're more likely to buy something if you touch it? There's a good reason why car salesmen say "a feel of the wheel will seal the deal"; why men fall in love with women who accidentally touch their shoulder; and why stores display products you can touch to your heart's content while leaving the rest in boxes to prevent your dirty mitts from handling them. Touching sends off the feeling of ownership and makes you think that you must buy it, whether or not you really need it.

0% Interest On Debt

Some people find themselves in debt up to their waist and the interest rate, which can be as much as 20%, is just rubbing salt in the wound. With this hack you'll be paying down a debt using a 0% interest credit card. Many credit cards offer an initial promotion of 0% interest for up to 18 months. If you're in considerable debt and plan to pay back the credit card company within the 0% interest period, go ahead and get a new credit card. You will need to have a good credit score to get one and your credit score will take a hit when you open the card. But this is nothing compared to an unpayable debt with an outrageous interest rate.

You Are Actually Three People—Visualize Your Future Self

Am I on drugs? No. Well... maybe. But there are actually three versions of ourselves throughout our lifetime—the past self, the present self, and the future self. We often think of our future self as a distant stranger that is somewhat irrelevant to us at the moment. I'm not just making this up; numerous studies have shown that visualizing our future self can make us save significantly more money. So go ahead and have a conversation with your future self and see what they have to say about your stupid spending decisions.

Free And Easy Coupons

If you're a coupon connoisseur then forget that stack of coupons you've been collecting for weeks. There is no point sorting through all of the mess trying to find the one you need or wasting time cutting up a newspaper. In the 21st century we have a little something known as the internet. With a two second Google search for coupon websites, you can be printing off the coupons you want for almost anything.

Bonus Tip: You can download coupon apps on your smartphone and access coupons from anywhere. Apps like Offer Beam use mobile technology to scan nearby stores in your location and send discounts straight to your phone!

View Spending As Hours Worked

If you're about to buy something that you don't really need, use this simple technique to control your spending habits. Calculate your hourly take-home pay and figure out how many hours you would have to work to pay for that item. This helps to put your spending into perspective and if you do buy it, you'll appreciate it more. Go ahead and try it anyway. You'll be amazed how fast things start to lose their appeal when you attach labor to it.

Buy Gift-Cards At A Huge Discount—For Yourself

Ever wondered what ungrateful people do with their unwanted gift cards? They sell them on the good ole internet for much less than they were purchased to people who would appreciate them. Sites such as GiftCardGranny, CardCash, and CardHub are swarming with cheap gift cards for people like you and me. You'll look like Bill Gates giving these cards out as gifts at Christmas time. Or better yet, keep them for yourself and go on a shopping spree the next time your favorite shop has a store-wide sale.

ABOUT THE AUTHOR

Damien Cash is the founder of Pryde Publishing. He is a life hacker, businessman, author, entrepreneur, and a time-traveling ninja with distant family ties to Superman. Mr. Cash has nine sons and seven daughters and dreams of starting his own family football team someday, although he does find his child support fees to be a major responsibility. He takes a light-hearted approach to everything and strongly believes we all need to take charge of our own lives, become our own boss, and "stick it to the Man".

www.ingramcontent.com/pod-product-compliance
Lightning Source LLC
Chambersburg PA
CBHW051300170526
45165CB00004B/1794